Remembrance and Gratitude

A Selection of Poems and Writings

by

Charles F. Meek

CCB Publishing
Terrace, British Columbia, Canada

Remembrance and Gratitude: A Selection of Poems and Writings

Copyright ©2013 by Charles F. Meek
ISBN-13 978-1-77143-071-5
First Edition

Library and Archives Canada Cataloguing in Publication
Meek, Charles F., 1943-
Remembrance and gratitude : a selection of poems and writings /
written by Charles F. Meek.
ISBN 978-1-77143-071-5
Also available in print format.
Additional cataloguing data available from Library and Archives Canada

All poems, essays and photos contained herein are copyright Charles F. Meek.

Extreme care has been taken by the author to ensure that all information presented in this book is accurate and up to date at the time of publishing. Neither the author nor the publisher can be held responsible for any errors or omissions. Additionally, neither is any liability assumed for damages resulting from the use of the information contained herein.

All rights reserved. No part of this publication may be reproduced, stored in a retrieval system or transmitted in any form or by any means, electronic, mechanical, photocopying, recording or otherwise without the express written permission of the publisher, except by a reviewer who may quote brief passages in a review to be printed in a newspaper, magazine, or journal. Printed in the United States of America, the United Kingdom and Australia.

Publisher: CCB Publishing
             Terrace, British Columbia, Canada
             www.ccbpublishing.com

Foreword

Over the years we have had the privilege of knowing Charlie and to appreciate his poetic genius. He has captured a wide spectrum of topics, both local and worldly; he has a particular love for his native Scotland, the land of his birth.

Our relationship with Charlie began many years ago with his radio show, *A Touch O' White Heather*, and also his Remembrance Day program hosted from our Tillicum Twin Theatres located here in Terrace, BC.

He is dedicated to the people of our community and the Royal Canadian Legion, helping bereaved families. Our association over the years has been, and still to this day is an enjoyable one. We are now pleased to present the fruits of his works, which are published in this book. We know that you will enjoy these wonderful poems and writings.

Bill and Norma Young
Terrace, BC

Praise for *Remembrance and Gratitude*

I have known Charles "Charlie" F. Meek for some time; from his days working for the Kitimat-Stikine Regional District as a Bylaw and Animal Control Officer, a radio celebrity, marriage commissioner, property manager, working with Coroner Services, and yes as a tax payer, but most importantly to me as a friend for almost 30 years.

Over the years I have listened to Charlie on the radio with his *A Touch O' White Heather* program or when not able to attend the Remembrance Day services in Terrace to his coverage of it over the radio. I have watched him officiate a marriage ceremony at our fire hall, and also officiate at numerous funerals for veterans, friends and firefighters.

As a firefighter and Fire Chief I have had the privilege to help protect the community and Charlie's home from wildfire, respond to medical emergencies, educate the public and train new firefighters. Charlie has thanked our fire department and shown his and Eleanor's appreciation by writing about our volunteer fire department and its members, and by coming to the fire hall and having a coffee and sharing a story or two.

When I read Charlie's poems about our fire department and its members I am reminded of past Chiefs Art Hill, Cal Albright and Ron Gerow and the hours they dedicated volunteering their time to make a better community and the friendships formed.

I hope you, the reader, enjoy these poems and prose and can relate to the community around you, wherever that may be.

Charles Wesley (Wes) Patterson
Fire Chief, Thornhill Fire Department

Preface

The poems and writings in this book are mostly dedications to friends and loved ones, as well as to our veterans, who sadly there are fewer as each year passes.

My wife Eleanor has inspired me in my writings, also two very dear friends, Bill and Norma Young, who are responsible for the publication of this book. My local fire department always enjoys my writings and dedications too.

I hope you will enjoy the contents, and picture in your mind the places I write about.

Charlie Meek

Contents

Foreword iii
Praise for *Remembrance and Gratitude* iv
Preface v
Norma and Bill Young 1
Eleanor, My Pride and Joy 2
A Mother's Son 3
As A Boy 5
Tribute to Mrs. Vesta Douglas, Freeman of the City of Terrace 7
No Tears or Goodbyes 9
Kleanza Creek 10
Tribute to My Friend Les Sinnott 12
Edna McConachie, A Very Special Lady 13
The Men and Women in Blue 15
The Old Man 16
Your Last Ride Home (Don't Drink and Drive) 18
Tribute to Albert DeJong 20
Do You Remember? 21
He's My Brother 23
Our Takysie Lake 25
My Flower the Rose 27
Back in Time 28
Our Little Angel, Kalila 29
History in the Making 31
John Mason, M.B.E. 32
Royal Canadian Legion Terrace Branch 13 34

We Can't Forget	35
My Relay for Life	37
Otto Lindstrom, My Friend	38
My Hawkair	40
Bob Grier, M.B.E.	42
Our Ladies of Mercy, Mills Memorial Hospital, Terrace, BC	44
Destiny	45
A Proud Coal Miner's Son	46
Thornhill Fire Hall	48
A Man I Know Well, Charles Wesley Patterson	50
In Memory of Fireman Ron Gerow	51
In Memory of Fireman Art Hill	53
In Memory of Fireman Cal Albright	55
A Fire Hall Christmas	56
A Quiet Time	58
Gordie's Tribute for His Sister-in-Law	59
Dedication from Slim Higgins to Charlie Meek	60
My Farewell to Otto Lindstrom	61
Tribute to My Friend Roy LeBlond	63
Tribute to My Friend Ron Mathews	65
Uncle Bob's Reward	66
Have You Ever Wondered?	68
A Special Thank You	69
Some Additional Poems	70
About the Author	71

Norma and Bill Young

Out here in the west, you will meet people who are simply the best
They come from all walks of life, often with laughter and jest
Some you will meet, they will stick in your mind
I know of two, two of the best, yes they are my kind.

Norma and Bill, live here in my town, they are known so well
I'm glad they are my friends, when you see us, you can tell
To me, they give me inspiration, to do the things that I do
My writings and my poems, I give to all of you.

The things they do for our town, they are, two of the best,
I'm proud to call them my friends, in their home, I am their guest
A welcome will await you, a coffee in your hand
Bill and Norma to me, are just simply grand.

One day soon, he will write the story of his life
This couldn't be done, without his loving wife
In his readings you will see, a legacy to be left behind
I am proud they are my friends, yes they are my kind.

I give a special thanks, for being my dear friends
If I can do for you, I freely will to no end.

Remembrance and Gratitude

Eleanor, My Pride and Joy

I've traveled this wide country, all across this great land
And met many people, and shook a welcome hand
But none more so than a lady, who was to be my life
And that loving lady, my ever loving wife.

We've been to many places, and traveled to places within reach
There's no place we love better, than our Hawaiian beach
It was there not so long ago, we joined our loving hands
We were joined together, on our fingers, golden bands.

She stands beside me, when I am feeling low
I see that childish grin, then I am all aglow
We have our lives to live, and friends to share it with
We have our ups and downs, we also have our bliss.

She is not just my wife, but a friend very true
And is not just there for me, but also for you
She is the love of my life, a joy to behold
And together we shall be, as we do grow old.

Charles F. Meek

A Mother's Son

I always wanted to be a soldier, just like my Dad
That's what his Mum said, about her bonnie wee lad
The years went by, he grew up strong
And still in the Army, is where Jamie longed.

The day came when Jamie sailed away
His Mum on the shore, praying he'd return one day
Jamie wrote to his darlin' Mum
Hello Mum, this is Jamie your loving son.

The guns are loud, the cannons are screaming
Coming home is what I'm dreaming
I can hear the pipes, I can hear them playing
We're coming home, they seem to be saying.

The pipes they played for a soldier's son
Who fought the battle, and fought and won
Jamie's Mum at the station was waiting
A pain in her heart, the tension was creating.

The crowd that gathered to see their village son
All were there for Jamie's Mum
The pipes were playing *The Battles O'er*
As the train pulled in, they opened the carriage door.

The flag draped coffin, was carried shoulder high
As the rifles fired into a cloudless sky
Jamie's home, he was one of the best
The pipes were playing, as he was laid to rest.

Remembrance and Gratitude

A soldier he was, from the cradle to the grave
For his country's freedom, his life he gave
Jamie's home, he was one of the best
The pipes were playing, as Jamie was laid to rest.

Charles F. Meek

As A Boy

Often I think back to when I was a boy, oh so many years ago
Playing as a child in the fields, and in the winter snow
Memories of those days, linger in my heart
One day I will return, to where my childhood did start.

In the old tower, where Bruce once fought
Looking over to Stirling, to where the English, Wallace caught
Raiding the Minister's apples, and Mum making an apple pie
Old Tom Kettles the cop, would catch us, often make us cry.

Those were the days when life was full of fun
Playing with our friends, at catch and run
Daffodils were my flower, and many I had
Often I got caught stealing, I guess I was bad.

Dad was a coal miner, deep down in the ground
He'd carry me on his shoulders, happiness was all around
Life was tough in those days, when every penny counted
War was on, the enemy surrounded.

Remembrance and Gratitude

So many of our friends, have passed away
Their memories linger on, even to this day
Oh I wish I was a child again, back in my childhood days
Back in my village, back in our old quaint ways.

Clackmannan was my home, where I grew up
And my little dog, I got as a pup
We'd roam around together, with not a care around
One day I will be, to Scotland I'll be bound.

Charles F. Meek

Tribute to Mrs. Vesta Douglas Freeman of the City of Terrace

In the springtime of her youth, she had a childish grin
The door to her home would be open, and she would welcome you in
Sit down over there, rest easy for a while
As she handed you a coffee, with that grin and a smile.

She is loved by many, disliked by none
She is every child's favourite Mum
The joy in her giving could be seen in her eyes
As she looks out her window, to the heavenly skies.

To know her is a pleasure, to not is a sin
Remember her door is open, and a welcome to come on in
Take her a bunch of flowers, or a candy or two
She will gladly share them, with me and with you.

In her twilight years, she rests unable to roam
The staff looks after her, in her Terraceview home
Her body is tired, feeble and old
Her mind is active, this you will be told.

So join with me and raise your glass
As we toast our Lady, Mrs. Douglas
She is a credit to one and to all
In her youth she stood proud, and she stood tall.

God looks down upon you this very day
And cares for you in every way
He knows all about you, for He has been told
Look out for our Vesta, proud, beautiful and bold.

Charles F. Meek

No Tears or Goodbyes

Don't be angry with me, because I didn't say goodbye
I know you all gather here, with a tear in your eye
I am now at peace, my fears of life now gone
Remember the good times, when we sang a merry song.

I ask for your forgiveness, for what I did do
Wherever I am, I will look down upon all of you
I ask you to remember me, for the love we all had
Please give each other a hug, please don't be sad.

Life must go on, carry on what I left undone
Give hope to a father, a son, and someone's Mum
You all have a gift, a gift you must share
I will look down upon you, I will always be there.

Dedicated to the memory of
Tracy Layton, M.M.H.

Kleanza Creek

There's a place we call home, a second one I guess
To Kleanza Creek in the summertime, with our motor home no less
To see our friends Gord and Carol, they are indeed two of the best.

Sitting by the fire, drinking coffee with Gord and Carol
Is what we love the best
Kleanza is not far for us to travel to
We get there and set up, and enjoy the things we do.

It is peace and tranquility, the quietness of the night
Just to hear the sounds of the water, flowing by is just right
If you happen to be down our way
Pop into Kleanza Creek, stay a while, and enjoy your stay.

Our host Gord, better known as muffin, and Carol his ever loving wife
Are two of the best, and take away the strife
They make us so welcome, with laughter and joy
She drives around in her buggy, which is her little toy.

Charles F. Meek

So come to Kleanza, stay and have some fun
Whether it is rainy or cloudy or fair, often you may see the sun
Perhaps to catch some fish, but you have to let them go
This is our Kleanza Creek, to us our second home
For we have Kleanza, Kleanza our second home.

Remembrance and Gratitude

Tribute to My Friend Les Sinnott

You lived your life to the fullest, and gave everything you had
As your children would say, you were the greatest Dad
You were always there when needed, with words to ease our pain
That's why you were our Dad, that was our gain.

Helping others in many different ways
From soccer to the Legion, you always had your say
Not just my friend, but many friends in your life
And most of all, you were the husband, to your darling wife.

We often promise to do things, some left undone
You were always there for us girls, and also for our Mum
Your words of wisdom and laughter will be no more
We never said goodbye, as you left and closed the door.

You were taken from us without warning
We will miss your big smile, as often seen in the morning
We will never forget of what, and who you are
As we look to the heavens, and see a brand new star.

Rest in Peace My Dear Friend
The Memories of You, Will Always Remain.

Charles F. Meek

Edna McConachie, A Very Special Lady

I write these words with a Lady in mind
She was so gentle, and the motherly kind
You see I met this Lady, just a few short years past
The memories I have, will forever last.

Edna was a Lady, so vibrant and sprite
She loved to travel, and travel was her right
We went to far off places, with a goal to be found
And to bonnie Scotland, Edinburgh we were bound.

We tramped the Highlands of Scotland, where the heather grows wild
I gave her a sprig o' heather, I pulled from the mountainside
She looked at me, with a smile on her face
She took that sprig o' heather, next to her heart it was placed.

She was a special Lady, and not just to me
All who met her, her friendship she gave free
A mother to her children, whom she loved with all her might
Each night she prayed, she said a loving good night.

Remembrance and Gratitude

In her twilight years, a legacy she left behind
In her writings and poems, that were written in a clear mind
Now we are left, with just the words she wrote
Edna has gone, we are left heart broke.

The memories we have when you were here
Will be held close to our hearts, ever so dear
We will think of you each day, for you are very special
You are with us we know, for you my dear, are our Guardian Angel.

Charles F. Meek

The Men and Women in Blue

Why oh why, do we have to cry
Why, tell me why, do they have to die
They protect us, from dangers in life
Every day they take it in stride.

They are our Police, the men and women in blue
They look out, for me, and for you
Far too many give their lives
We grieve for their families, and their wives.

Many years ago, in my hometown
A coward took an officer down
He was doing his duty, to protect us all,
His comrades watched, and saw Michael fall.

We remember him, as the years go by
We shed a tear, and salute the officer who died
When you see them, on the road
Give them a wave, it lightens their load.

Give them thanks, and lots of praise
As they go about their daily ways
They are your friends, each and every one
Make sure they come home, to their loved ones.

Many are my friends, the men and women in blue
I hold out my hand in friendship, to each one of you
And pray for your safety, and give you a wave
As I pass you on the street, and pray you come home safe.

Dedicated to the memory of Michael Buday

Remembrance and Gratitude

The Old Man

It was a dark and dreary wet night
When the old man I saw, I caught sight
I walked up to him and offered my hand
Can I help you my friend, I took my stand.

He replied in a croaked voice, I am fine and thank you my friend
I am going to the park, a bench for the night, I will find
I couldn't let this man, on this Christmas Eve
Sleep in the park, in the cold he would freeze.

I took him to a motel, and gave him a room for the night
Here my friend, is my gift to you this night
The old man looked with a tear in his eye
I don't mind sleeping, under God's heavenly sky.

I thank you for this gift you give,
Sleeping in parks, is where I lived
This night I will sleep, in a warm clean bed
And on the pillow I will rest my head
I bade him goodnight, and said I will see you on the morrow
It will be Christmas Day, there will be no sorrow.

I went to see the old man, to take him for a meal
The doctor he beat me, the old man's heart did not heal
He left this world, with a smile on his face
For he died in comfort, and full of grace.

In his old suitcase, papers were found
Many medals of all kinds, in an old rag, they were bound
For this was an old soldier, of misfortune he died
I stood at his bed, and silently, I cried.

Charles F. Meek

Rest in peace, my old friend
I am happy you had a peaceful end
This world is grateful, for what you had done
A soldier, a veteran, and second to none
May you be in Heaven, this Christmas night
The battle is over, you fought the good fight.

Your Last Ride Home
(Don't Drive and Drive)

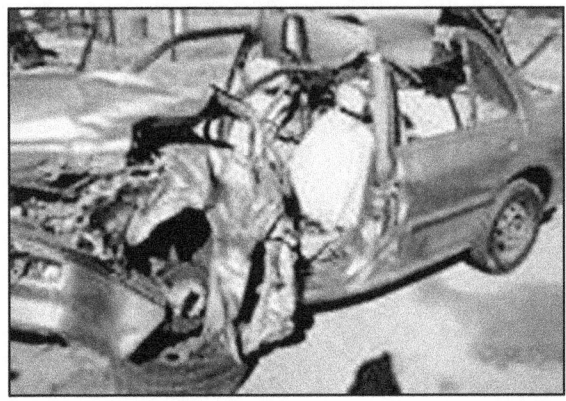

To you who graduate, and ready to join the fold
Please drink wisely, and live to be old
Designate a driver, don't make it a race
Arrive home safely, so your family can see your smiling face.

Life is so precious, and too much to lose
Don't let it all end, all because of the booze
Think beforehand, of the ones you leave behind
Arrive home safely, to your family's peace of mind.

If not you who is damaged, think of the ones you will cause pain
Perhaps not your family, just someone in a picture frame
You have graduated, to enjoy a full life
Take everything as it comes, even life's strife.

Don't let me be, your last ride home
Think wisely, and the world is yours to roam
You see, my work, is full of sadness and pain
Don't let your passing, be the Devil's gain.

Charles F. Meek

Please don't drink and drive
Drink wisely, and please grow old
Bring new life into this world, with laughter and fun
Don't let me be your last ride home, don't let me be your last run.

Remembrance and Gratitude

Tribute to Albert DeJong

In this world, there are folks who I've come across
Some come and go, and some who have been lost
One such friend, a cut above the other
Albert is his name, I was proud to call Brother.

He loved to fish the river, and the ocean blue
He always had time, for folks like me and you
Hunting and ski-dooing, down the snowy slopes
Pulling that big moose, all tied up in ropes.

He was a loving father, his family was his life
His children, and yes, his adoring wife
Life was so wonderful, the world was at his hand
What he believed in, he would make a firm stand.

If you had his friendship, you could do no wrong
That man was a brother, he was, our Albert DeJong
You would see him in his truck, driving down the road
Little did we know, he was carrying a heavy load.

He bore his burden bravely, and so full of grace
And when you saw him, he had a smile on his face
Albert has now gone, to his Heaven above
He left this world, he also left his love.

Albert was a good man, and one of a kind
Keep his memory with you, keep him in your mind
I am proud that I knew him, I am proud he was a friend
We will always remember him, we will, until our end.

Charles F. Meek

Do You Remember?

Do you remember, not so long ago, when life was full of fun?
We would visit the beach, and along the pristine sands we would run
We would go for summer drives, along the country roads
Just to relax, and ease of the burdensome loads.

Those were the days, when friends we would meet
Shaking hands, giving hugs, and a friendly greet
In the wintertime we would gather around the fire
And wish it was springtime, that is our desire.

To see the flowers bloom, the roses and the daffodils
And hear the birds a singing, it was such a thrill
Now we're old, and getting on in years
We recall the laughter and fun, and yes often the tears.

We built ourselves a cabin, in the forest glade
Going for the weekends, and the fires we made
It was fun in those days, just you and I
We'd sit by the fire, and look at the night time sky.

Remembrance and Gratitude

Oh if only those days could come back, and live them again
Happiness would be ours to dream of now and then
Now in our twilight years, we sit by the fire
Dreaming of those days gone by, to relive them is our desire.

Charles F. Meek

He's My Brother

Often in our lifetime a special person comes along,
Even when they are gone the memory lingers on
Such is in the case of a man I called my Brother,
Friendship was our goal, friends to one another.

You see Ron was a big man with a big heart to match,
Laurie was his wife a perfect match
His kids all grew up and went their own way,
But their loving Dad was never far away.

He was a First Nations man, and proud that he was,
He would go fishing in the Skeena from his home at Gitaus
He is my big brother, and a proud man
I am to have Ron beside me as often as I can.

Our time on earth is short lived each day to the best,
Just a few short years ago, my brother went to his rest
Our hearts were all broken at Ron going away,
We wish he could be with us, we wish he could stay.

Remembrance and Gratitude

> Even tho' he has gone, and in Heaven above
> He will always be my brother, a brotherly love
> We all really do miss you and think of you each day,
> You are my big brother and in my heart you will stay.

Dedicated to the memory of Ron Mould.

Charles F. Meek

Our Takysie Lake

In the early morning when the sun is rising,
We look over the lake over to the horizon
All is quiet not a sound to be heard,
All but the loon, as his wings he does spread.

He takes off in flight across our pleasant lake,
As he gives chase to the lonesome drake
This is our Takysie Lake.

Our hosts David and Rise in our piece of Heaven,
Is equal to all our lucky sevens
We play in the evening a game of cards,
With Eleanor, Bob, and Linda, Bob's my pard.

We play for dimes and all he takes,
We're here, here at our Takysie Lake
In the twilight of the night the reflection of the moon,
shimmering over the lake
The eerie sound of the loon as he cries, looking for his mate.

Remembrance and Gratitude

Watching the eagles soar swooping down to catch their prey,
The fish that swim on freely, the eagles take away
There is a group of ducks that come to us for food,
To see them is so pleasant to picture them so good.

We take the boat out and troll for fish, or just to have a break
This is our piece of Heaven, this is our Takysie Lake.

And so our time here is at an end
Down the road we go turning at every bend
We shall return in days to come,
Back to Takysie to see the morning sun.

With us we go with the movies we make,
Of our beloved Takysie Lake.

Charles F. Meek

My Flower the Rose

I sat down to think, of how I can picture you
And thought of all the flowers, that grow in the morning dew
There is the Golden Daffodil, that sways in the breeze
And think of you, as you always wish to please.

And then there is the Snowdrop, small and snow white
The smile that you smile, cheers up our life
Then the Yellow Primrose, that flutters in the wind
It shows off your nature, so gentle and so kind.

And the Scottish Bluebell, that stands firm and tall
I will always be there, should you ever fall
The Rhododendron , so majestic and grand
That's why we're proud of you, you always make your stand.

The flower that embellishes you, bears your loving name
Many colours, many names, and many of great fame
You are my favourite Aunt, and we are very close
That's why you're my flower, my own Special Rose.

Dedicated to Debbie's Aunt Rose

Remembrance and Gratitude

Back in Time

If I could turn the clock back, to many years long ago
I wouldn't be in mourning, for all the friends I know
All our loving soldiers, would be with their families this day
I wouldn't need to wear my poppy, this Remembrance Day.

If I could turn the clock back, to the time when life was fun
We wouldn't have to fear the violence, we wouldn't have to run
Instead we could be friends, and share the happy times
And sing the good old songs, and all keep in rhyme.

If I could turn the clock back, even to the days of our youth
Of how we could change the world, and listen to the truth
To see the waters flow, from the rivers and the streams
To the big blue ocean, where they carry all our dreams.

But then if I turned the clock back, to that time long ago
Would I be here today, would I even know you?
I'm glad the clocks go back, for just an hour this time
I am your friend, and I am happy you are mine.

I can't turn the clock back, to those many years ago
Today we have conflicts, and the poppies, grow and grow
And this November the 11th, I will wear my poppy red
And say a prayer for our fallen heroes, as I sleep safely in my bed.

Charles F. Meek

Our Little Angel, Kalila

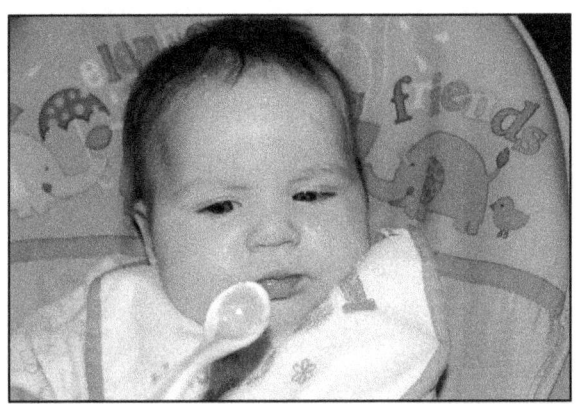

There is a beautiful little girl, who changed our life
She is very special, to me and my wife
She came into this world, not long ago
And when she smiles, we are all aglow.

Happiness is mine, when she sits on my knee
All you have to do, is just look and see
She comes to visit me and her Gran
Her Dad, he is our main man.

And Gail, her Mum, is a special lady too
She loves our little girl, if only you knew
Kalila is her name, our own little pride and joy
And me, I'm as happy as any little boy.

We've never been grandparents before
It's like God brought her to us, to our front door
We care and love this little girl so much
Her smile is heavenly, her skin, gentle to the touch.

Remembrance and Gratitude

She is our Kalila, our bonnie wee girl
Each time we see her, a wondrous thrill
Grandma and Grandpa, love her so dear
We will watch her grow up, we will always be here.

Charles F. Meek

History in the Making

It has been seven hundred years, since Bruce was the King
When he fought for our freedom, for all our kith and kin
On the field at Bannockburn, the year 1314
Victory was in sight, to the Scots this could be seen.

For many years, we have been ruled, ruled from down south
Freedom was spoken, spoken, by word and mouth
Time went by, and wars had been fought
Side by side, the enemy was sought.

History is in the making, freedom can be made
Seven hundred years later, the Scots can have their say
We can sing our national anthem, and sing it with pride
The Flower of Scotland, we will sing, side by side.

Choose wisely for your freedom, make every voice count
Scotland can be ours, this I have no doubt
Sing The Flower of Scotland, with voices loud and clear
With voices that can be heard, freedom is so near.

Listen to the pipes, as they play our favourite songs
Seeking our freedom, speak freely, for it is not wrong
Bonnie Scotland, you are my home
To foreign lands I will no longer roam.

Remembrance and Gratitude

John Mason, M.B.E.

Today we are sad, as we say goodbye to a dear friend
Music was his life, he pleased us to the end
John Mason and the famous S.F.O.
Was well known, throughout the world, this we know.

It is not goodbye, as his music lives on
Nothing was too much, for John to be put upon
He wrote many tunes, and were pleasant to hear
Dancing in the Isles, with your partner near.

He wrote a tune for Eleanor and me
A polka to play, happiness was ours, this you could see
The memories we have of John and the S.F.O.
We keep and will never let go.

Hilary and John's hospitality, when we visited their home
Is ours to keep, wherever we roam
The fun and laughter could be heard in the street
The music at their house, where all friends would meet.

Charles F. Meek

This is not a goodbye, just cheerio for now
We will all meet again, when and where, I don't know how
Play your music, in Heaven above
And remember, here on Earth, you are loved.

Play your music in Heaven above, where the Angels will be your choir
Meet all those who have gone before you, I promise we won't cry.
The Flower of Scotland will bloom no more
For Auld Lang Syne, and Caddam Wood, we all take the floor.

Remembrance and Gratitude

Royal Canadian Legion Terrace Branch 13

I am a member of Legion Branch Thirteen
In the City of Terrace, we can be seen
We look after our veterans, this is our decree
So come on in, a welcome awaits, for you and for me.

There are many faces that you will get to know
From the President and Directors, the smiles all aglow
And you will have a chance to meet, a lady from command
Where she will welcome you, with an open hand.

You see Branch 13 history did make
A member, Dominion President, she did make
We are very proud, of Mary-Ann, and her great esteem
For she has done lots, for all of us at Branch Thirteen.

Our aim is to help all our vets, and pay tribute to everyone
Although they grow old, they are the best, next to none
At the end of their days, a tribute we make
A full Honour to their lives we all partake.

Yes I am proud to be a Legion Member
For what it has done for me, I will always remember
So come on in, and join this great Branch
And become a member, and lend a helping hand.

Charles F. Meek

We Can't Forget

It's that time of year again, when we gather at the mall
We all march proudly, beside the veterans, who gave their all
Now they have grown old, and in their twilight years
In days long gone by, they fought with no fears.

We wear our blood red poppies, and wear them with pride
Their valour we will never forget, for them we abide
Give praise to those who gave us freedom, for that we enjoy
Never forget, that man, that woman, and the young boy.

Many years have gone by, from the great wars they fought
They came from all walks of life, their courage they brought
From First Nations villages, they left their loved ones dear
Fought alongside their brothers, with no fear.

Those brave men and women, from all walks of life
By land, sea and air, they took it in stride
Let us remember those who fell, and those who gave their lives
Their names etched in stone, memorized with great pride.

Remembrance and Gratitude

So this November the 11th, please pause for a moment or two
Remember those men and women, they gave freedom to me and you
And give praise to those who are still with us, this Remembrance Day
Give them peace and tranquility, for this we all pray.

Charles F. Meek

My Relay for Life

Today is a day that we celebrate, a day I proudly walk with you
You fought the valiant battle, and I fought it with you
Many tears were shed, when we got the news, of the illness you had
All our plans for the future, we put them to the back.

We took each step, slowly, and slowly, day by day
Each night I laid in bed, each night I did pray
For a miracle, anything, a cure has to be found
And so to Vancouver, the big city we were bound.

The hands of the surgeon, were guided by our prayers
As he took away your illness, and eased both our fears
The road to recovery, will be a step-by-step
All our friends are with you, this we won't forget.

And today we all walk together, for we won the valiant fight
Let's all look forward to tomorrow, good health is in our sight
Today I walk proudly, in this Relay for Life
Today I walk proudly, at the side of my loving wife.

Never give up the battle, stay positive all the way
It is a fight we won, and did it day by day
Today I walk proudly, with each and everyone
Tomorrow we will all see, the rising of the sun.

I walk proudly, with you all, and with my dear wife
Today I walk proudly, in this Relay for Life.

Dedicated to my wife Eleanor Meek

Otto Lindstrom, My Friend

He's ninety-five years old, and still drives his little car
Just around our town, and places not too far.
We often go for coffee, just to pass the time of day
He is a terrific person, of this I am happy to say.

Many years ago, as a young man he was
He fought in the war, he fought for a great cause
Rarely does he talk, of those days long gone by
He looks up to the heavens, and just gives a sigh.

Each November the eleventh, you can see him proudly stand
Marching proudly, to the music, the music of the band
He wears a blood red poppy, as he remembers his fallen friends
He remembers each year, this he will continue, to no end.

You will see him around town, selling you a poppy red
Wear it and give thanks, each night you go to bed
It was people like Otto, who gave you your freedom today
If you see him around, say Sir, can I shake your hand, if I may?

Charles F. Meek

You see my friend Otto, is a wonderful friend to know
When he calls for coffee, I look forward to go
He is now in his twilight years, and slow as he walks
His memory is perfect, I know that when he talks.

I give him praise, because he is Otto, my friend.

My Hawkair

I have traveled this fair land, and been to many places
I've seen the big cities, and many strange faces
I've flown in many planes, some big and some small
My favourite is Hawkair, the best of them all.

The folks at Hawkair, are great and so kind
And if my flight is delayed, really, I don't mind
They support our town, in more ways than one
They are the best, and second to none.

The staff at the airports, assist in every way
They listen to the moans and groans, and to the dismays
They smile and listen, and ease those pains, the best way they can
The folks at Hawkair, are great, every woman and every man.

We support our local airline, as they do for us
And try to avoid a cancellation, and avoid taking the bus
If you need a quick flight, and need to be there quick
I choose Hawkair, that is my number one pick.

Charles F. Meek

For ten years now, Hawkair has flown from our hometown
Above that flying logo, I would love to place a crown
To everyone at Hawkair, I hold out my hand
And pray you continue, to fly our fair land.

From me to you, I wish you the best
Pleasing your customers, is your ultimate quest
From the pilots and ground crew
My hand in friendship is extended to you.

Remembrance and Gratitude

Bob Grier, M.B.E.

I write this, of a man I know best
In Largoward his head he rests
He is so well known, by friends and kin
At the village hall, you will be welcomed in.

For many years not long ago, he would stand at the door
Then you could hear him call, ladies and gentlemen, take the floor
Sir Jimmy is on stage, for an eightsome reel
Take your partners, a Scottish welcome, you will feel.

Uncle Bob has had the best, playing the hall with music in mind
Come on in, and great music you'll find
There's Sir Jimmy, and Bobby Crowe
Billy Anderson, whom you all know.

And of course there's Faither, who plays so grand
And young Bruce, the son of the man
He's had so many great bands of old
Their music is well known, you will be told.

Charles F. Meek

With Aunt Margaret on a Saturday night
A cup of tea, and a snawba, is just right
Uncle Bob is so revered, this I do know well
The folks of Largoward, this they will tell.

Not too long ago, he got the M.B.E.
For the work he did, for you and me
We're proud of this gentle man
He's our Uncle, and that is just grand.

So lift your glass, as we toast his health
We the people, are his wealth
From Eleanor and Charlie, in a far off land
Proudly love you, and shake your hand.

Remembrance and Gratitude

Our Ladies of Mercy
Mills Memorial Hospital, Terrace, BC

There is a group of ladies, and gentlemen too
Who dedicate their time to me and to you
They work in my local hospital, here in my hometown
They are the folks of Mills Memorial, you never see them frown.

If you are in their care, as someday you may well be
You will gently be cared for, just wait and see
The doctors and nurses from all walks of life
Are always here to help you, that is their pride.

There are too many names to mention, maybe just a few
There is Cheryl, a laugh a minute, a smile she will give to you
Then Pat is on the phone, making sure everything is good
Ensuring of your comfort, right down to the food.

I often work with the folks here, here at Mills Memorial
I am proud to call you my friends, I know you give your all
So don't worry about the care, that you will receive
It will be the best, that they will give to thee.

A simple thank you, to them for what they do
A box of chocolates, a bunch of flowers, especially from you
And so to you, who dedicate your life, to the patients in your care
I pray there isn't too much strife, and everything is okay there.

I am proud to call you my friends, I thank you for what you do
My hand is held out to thank you, this I gladly do.

Charles F. Meek

Destiny

What is to be my destiny...

Would I travel the world, to places never seen?
Would I meet people of great cultures, maybe meet the Queen?
Perhaps I will leave my mark, of things I would like to do
Maybe meet someone, someone just like you.

Perhaps I can help someone, who needs a helping hand
Comfort somebody who is sad, or walk drifting sands
I am sure our destiny, is marked out in our life
We have good days, and some full of strife.

We can tread safely, and be careful what we say
Take my hand, I will help you on your way
My goal in life, is to help one and all
I will be there, should you ever fall.

I have traveled the world, and been to places I'd never seen
And met many people, and also met the Queen
I am there for our veterans, who I proudly call my friends
And yes I have chatted, to people just like you to no end.

My destiny is not yet complete
There are still many people, of whom I hope to meet
If I can lend a helping hand, and share some thoughts with you
Lean on me, I am here, that is my destiny.

A Proud Coal Miner's Son

I am the son of a coal miner, and proud that I am
My Dad worked in the coal mines, to bring the coal up high
Along with my brothers, they worked at digging coal
John, Hugh and David, they gave their all.

Dad wouldn't let me work in those mines, deep down underground
He said that's not the place for you, I'll keep you above ground
Many friends gave their lives, to bring up that black gold
Many left those mines, and gracefully grew old.

The years in those mines, did take their toll
Dad, David and Hugh, never did grow old
John and me are left behind, to remember those dark years
With those who have gone, we did shed some tears.

Life goes on, we have to live
The mines and the coal, we give back to Mother Earth
Yes a miner's son, and proud I am to be
I'm glad I wasn't in those mines, my Dad he kept me free.

Charles F. Meek

> Now we are older, the mines are all gone
> We live our lives, and try to have fun
> Now we are two, just John and me
> And proud to be a coal miner's sons
> John and me, are very proud you see.

Dedicated in memory of my father, David Meek.

Thornhill Fire Hall

As a little boy I watched them go by
In their big red trucks, they seemed to fly
The lights are flashing red and white
Looking nice and bright in the dead of night.

They go to help someone in need
And drive by at a hasty speed
The men and women from my Thornhill Hall
Adrenalin flowing, they give their all.

They are my friends, each and every one
A mother, a father, a loving son
They answer the call without distaste
And meet the challenge, with full haste.

There's Ron and Ken and Judy too
Wes and Dave, just to name a few
I am proud of them every one
I pray they come home at the setting sun.

Charles F. Meek

If you see them at work or at play
Give them a wave, or a smile this day
Their efforts and dedications are not in vain
As they race to ease someone's pain.

Bless the one, and bless them all
The men and women from my Thornhill Hall
We salute you, I shake your hand,
You are my friends, to me that is just grand.

Remembrance and Gratitude

A Man I Know Well, Charles Wesley Patterson

I write of a man, of whom I am honoured to know
I've known him for many years, our friendship grows and grows
If you are in need of help, all you have to do is ask
Wes will be there, regardless of the task.

He is one of a kind, a community minded man
He does, what he does, and all that he can
I've known him for many years, much to my chagrin
His door is always open, a welcome to come on in.

A man with responsibility, Fire Chief of my hall
He and his crew, they work and give their all
Eleanor and I, treat him like our own, for he is very special to us
We do what we do, without any great fuss.

So if you see this friend of ours, hold out your hand
Greet him with sincerity, for he is our gentle man.

In Memory of Fireman Ron Gerow

Captain ring that bell, loud and clear
Today we have lost someone dear
He was called to Heaven above
He leaves behind, those he loved.

Ron was a friend, to one and all
He was there if you had a fall
He will be remembered, for his friendship true
His hand was held out, to me and to you.

Captain ring that bell, loud and clear
Today we have lost someone dear
Let us think of the good he has done
He was a mother's loving son.

His wife and family will miss him dearly
The memories, keep in your hearts clearly
His goal in life was to keep you safe
His love of life was his faith.

Remembrance and Gratitude

Captain ring that bell, loud and clear
Today we have lost someone dear.
Rest in Peace, in Heaven above
In friendship, you will always be loved.

Captain ring that bell, loud and clear
Today we have lost someone very dear.

In Loving Memory of
My Dear Friend
Ron Gerow
January 6th 2011

Charles F. Meek

In Memory of Fireman Art Hill

Chief I ask you to ring that bell, ring it once again
Another comrade has fallen, when will it all end
Fireman Hill, has left this world, to be with his loved one above
To be with his Pauline, the one he dearly loved.

Just a few short months ago, Pauline also left us behind
Art missed her dearly, she was always on his mind
He was a fireman in our Thornhill Hall
Also a past Chief, and yes he gave his all.

He left a legacy, to us all here today
His teachings, and his training, we do his way
Even tho' he has gone, his memory remains
Chief, ring that bell, ring it once again
Art left his friendship, for that we have gained.

His name will be placed in honour, beside Cal and Ron
It will be placed on the wall, so we may all look on
Each time you all go out on an emergency call
Art, Cal, and Ron will be looking on.

Remembrance and Gratitude

Chief ring that bell, one last time
And pray we don't hear it again
Ring it loud, and ring it clear
In memory of Fireman Hill
Who is close to us, and who is near.

Charles F. Meek

In Memory of Fireman Cal Albright

Chief, ring that bell once again, today we have lost another friend
Cal was a fireman for many years, today we stand with sorrowful tears
He was a stalwart in the work he did, for that he stood tall
He was a respected fireman, in our Thornhill Hall.

He was a friend to many, to some for many years
He did his fireman's job, with little fear
Cal has left this world, with much work undone
Helping others, like you and me, and having some fun.

But today we mourn his passing, the Lord called him above
Cal will fight no more fires, he leaves behind his love
Chief, ring that bell once again, today we have lost another friend
Cal fought a mighty battle, he fought it to the very end.

We will miss your laughter, and seeing you smile
You would help everyone, and go the last mile
Chief ring that bell, for you have lost a good friend
The memories you all have, keep them till the end.

A Fire Hall Christmas

Another year is over, Christmastime is near
We all gather to celebrate, and have a drink of good cheer
There are some members of my fire hall, who cause me some grief
Let me start, and start with the chief.

Now he knows I like my car toys
He got me in trouble, with a bloody Rolls Royce
He found it on the net, and showed me a pic
Eleanor told me, if I bought it, I could go live with Rick.

Then there is Pat, he sells a drink called Coke
Me I'm a Pepsi man, I don't care if he goes broke
Then there is Rick, a weatherman he should be
He predicted the snow, it came for all to see.

Now Broadway is a wee man, always a smile on his face
Always laughing, his jokes a disgrace
And Darlene works hard, at cleaning the chief's desk
In all honesty, it's always a mess.

Charles F. Meek

Sometimes we go out, have a coffee and a wee snack
I end up with the bill, I'm not bloody going back
The hall always buys things, from picks to axes
At least I know, I'm paying them with my taxes.

From Eleanor and I, we hold you in respect
The men and women in my hall, you are the absolute best
We wish you all a Merry Christmas, and full of good cheer
A safe one, and a very Happy New Year.

Remembrance and Gratitude

A Quiet Time

Another year almost done, it is all but gone
I thank the Lord, we didn't hear the bell gong
We do remember our fallen friends, who left us behind
Their names we will remember, and always will come to mind.

We all gather tonight, to have fun and good cheer
A wee dram for the ladies, and the men, a good beer
Presentations, to our firemen and women, for work well done
We are proud to be your friends, you are all second to none.

I often pop into the hall, for a coffee and a chat
I see something new, and ask the Chief, did I really buy that
I see all the work, and the training you do.
As always, I hold my hand out to you.

It is nice that once a year, we get to see you relax
Enjoy and have fun, you have earned it, that is a fact
I know we can sleep easy, and rest without fear
Knowing if we need you, you are close, and always near.

Charles F. Meek

Gordie's Tribute for His Sister-in-Law

It doesn't seem so long ago when you came into our fold
You made our lives into pleasant times, and stories to behold
You took the times, good and bad, and carried on your way
You still remained my favourite, as you are to this day.

The waters that flow to the river, and on to the deep blue sea
Is how I will remember, the memories of you and me
Soon you will be leaving, and peace to you will ever be
Leaving us with heartfelt sorrows, happiness to see you free
Your memory to us will never fade, this I want you to know.

God Bless, Godspeed, on your journey ahead
To see another like you, I know will never come
And when that day, the day we dread, and you join another fold
I will tell the stories, the stories, of love untold.

You see you are very special, even tho' you don't think you are
You soon will be in Heaven
My very own shining star.

Dedicated to the memory of Marie Muir, Eagle Bay, BC.

Remembrance and Gratitude

Dedication from Slim Higgins to Charlie Meek

A Touch O' White Heather and *Down in the Glen*
He's listened to by many, families and friends
Here on a Sunday, his program is heard
Spreading good humour, and a fine Scottish word.

At nine we all listen to hear Charlie say
We've come again Laddie, hear the pipes play
We've come here to greet you, so welcome my friend
To *A Touch O' White Heather*, and *Down in the Glen*.

To scenes in the orchard, with flags flying high
And the soft sounds of the bagpipes, come drifting in by
And the love of our music, we know never ends
A Touch O' White Heather, and *Down in the Glen*.

Now some say the Master will call as you know
We all here answer, we all have to go
And end our sufferings, yes we all make amends
With *A Touch O' White Heather* and *Down in the Glen*.

Charles F. Meek

My Farewell to Otto Lindstrom

Do you remember not too long ago
A gentle old man, gave you a poppy to go
That old man was a dear friend of mine
He had a heart of gold, was gentle and kind.

He was a veteran, from a war long past
To shake his hand, all you had to do was ask
He would ask, buy a poppy and wear it with pride
Remember the fallen, with them I abide.

No more will you see this old man, with the poppy tray
For he has gone, our hearts in dismay
An Angel came and spoke gently to my friend
Your life on earth, your deeds at an end.

You were on this earth for a very long time,
a journey now you must make
Come with me the Angel said,
and held out her hand, for Otto to take.

Remembrance and Gratitude

You left this world with no words of goodbye
Today with broken hearts, many tears we have cried.
Rest in peace, the memories are ours to keep
Rest in peace, in your everlasting sleep.

Charles F. Meek

Tribute to My Friend Roy LeBlond

He was a giant of a man, so gentle and kind
I stand here today, and say, I am proud, he was a friend of mine
We traveled many miles, on land and on the sea
In all kinds of weather, there was Roy and me.

He was a proud man, and loved his family dearly
All you had to do was listen, he spoke of them so clearly
If a helping hand was needed, you just gave Roy a call
He would be there to help, and he would give his all.

When we went fishing, to the Channel we would go
Put our lines over, as the boat swayed to and fro
I'd hear Roy shouting, a fish on the line
I had one on as well, but his, well it was bigger than mine.

And when you saw that smile, you knew everything was fine
And yes I say it again, I'm proud Roy was a friend of mine
Now he has gone, he left this world too soon
I look up to the heavens, I can see him, by the light of the moon.

Remembrance and Gratitude

>Often we worked together, side by side
>I took him from his home, my heart breaking
>As I was his last ride.

Charles F. Meek

Tribute to My Friend Ron Mathews

I write this of a friend, a friend true and dear
If you ever needed him, he was always close and near
He was a young man with a talent, and deemed to go places
He worked at my local bank, always remembered faces.

Often I would go in, and share a laugh or two
Ron would hear me, and call out, I knew it was you
We would stand and chat, pass the time of day
He helped me with my challenges, he showed me the way.

Yes, Ron Mathews was indeed one of the best.

One day we went to the ocean blue, to fish and have fun
To catch the ultimate halibut, Ron just wanted one
You see he never caught one before, this was my goal
To make sure he did this, a halibut on his pole.

Joy to behold my wish it came true
Here Ron, a halibut, a big one, just for you
Sadly it was his last time, on the ocean blue
An Angel called, and said Ron, I am coming for you.

Ron left this world, and left broken hearts
We remember him each year, as the Relay of Life starts.

Rest in Peace My Friend, you are always remembered.

Uncle Bob's Reward

Overlooking Largoward, a new day is dawning
It's a sad day for the village, as they are in mourning
Bob Grier, M.B.E. has gone to meet his maker
A gentle kind man, no one could be greater.

To be in his company, and learn the things he knew
The work he did in his youth, his likes are very few
The village hall on a Saturday night, where you danced the night away
Uncle Bob shouting, grab a partner, and make those hips sway.

We loved this gentle man, and Aunt Margaret too
He would give a helping hand, a hand to me and you
His garden full of flowers, which was his pride and joy
When Eleanor was a wee lass, he would build her a nice wee toy.

He was admired by the folks, the folks of Largoward
Also all the dance bands, who played at the hall
For Uncle Bob they played, they played, and gave their all
It was an honour to know him, he always stood so tall.

Charles F. Meek

Uncle Bob is now with the Angels, in Heaven above
Asleep, and now at peace, oh how he was loved
The legacy he left behind, he left nothing undone
Remember Uncle Bob, there will never be another one.

Have You Ever Wondered?

Have you ever wondered where Old Man Winter goes
When springtime comes, and new flowers grow
To see the snowdrops, creep through the melting snow
And the golden daffodil, a flower we all know.

To wake up in the morning, and hear the wild bird's song
I can see a beautiful day, in the early morning dawn
Peace and tranquility by the side of the babbling brook
Sitting in my chair, by the camp fire, reading my book.

The memories this creates are mine to keep
New friends come by, new friends to meet
Don't take each day for granted, live it to the fullest
Stop for a moment, and give a little thanks,
Mother Earth will take care of the rest.

Enjoy each season as it comes along, make every one the best
Yesterday is history, tomorrow is the future, today is a gift
That's why we call it, "The Present."

Charles F. Meek

A Special Thank You

You say you love my writings, and the words that I have wrote
Many of them are true, and to many I have spoke
I like to feel that you are with me, and live the words I write
Of the people who are dedicated, I think of them at night.

Many of the works, are of people, people who have gone
Les, Art, and Albert, and my close friend Ron
It is my way of remembering, a friendship I do miss
To the heavens I look, and blow them a nightly kiss.

I am pleased you enjoy, and understand what I say
Often of faraway places, places far away
To the land of my birth, where once I walked the land
I give you my hand in friendship, I ask you take my hand.

In years to come, when the Good Lord calls
I leave my words, to remember me by, I leave them to you all
I give thanks, to you, who have thanked me
My thanks to you, are in my writings for you to see.

If I can make someone happy, and a smile on their face
Your thoughts and comments, are so full of grace
I am your dear friend, and I am who I am
I will keep on writing, as long as I can.

Some Additional Poems

I hope you have enjoyed the poems and writings in the book. As you have read, I often officiate at funerals and memorial services for our veterans, and members of my branch at the Royal Canadian Legion, as well as for Remembrance Day services.

There are some poems I read at those services, even though I did not write them myself. The words of these poems accent the service. I have listed some of these poems below and provided a link so you may read them and enjoy their meanings.

When Tomorrow Starts Without Me
http://www.poeticexpressions.co.uk/POEMS/Iftomorrowstartswithoutme.htm

Letter from Heaven
http://unforgettableangels.angelstouch16.com/Letter/letter.htm

My First Christmas in Heaven
http://www.utahshare.org/newsletter/2012/11/01/1051/

The Old Comrade
http://www.rcl462.ca/old-comrade.html

Why Wear A Poppy
http://www.veterans.gc.ca/eng/feature/vetweek/comm_guide/poems

Merry Christmas, My Friend
http://www.hymnsandcarolsofchristmas.com/Poetry/merry_christmas_my_friend.htm

Just A Common Soldier
http://vaincourt.homestead.com/common_soldier.html

Sincerely yours,
Charlie

About the Author

Charles F. Meek has lived in Terrace, British Columbia ever since emigrating from Scotland in 1979. He is very involved in his community. Over the years he has been Commanding Officer of 747 Squadron of the local Air Cadets and past President of Royal Canadian Legion Branch 13.

Working for the Veterans was first and foremost, and he still hosts the Remembrance Day services from the Tillicum Twin Theatres on November 11th of each year, which is broadcast on CityWest's Community Channel 10. He has also hosted a Scottish radio show, *A Touch O' White Heather*, and television program, *Down in the Glen*. At one time Charlie was a Marriage Commissioner. He enjoyed seeing many happy people and has many fond memories.

Assisting others is a part of his life, and he continues helping people by serving at funeral and memorial services. Now semi-retired, Charlie enjoys fishing on the ocean with friends. Charlie is married to his wife Eleanor, who has inspired many of his poems and writings.

www.ingramcontent.com/pod-product-compliance
Lightning Source LLC
Chambersburg PA
CBHW031655040426
42453CB00006B/318